W9-AQV-795

Matthew Abess, editor
Mylinh Trieu Nguyen, art director
Lisa Li, coordinator
David Almeida, photographer
Lynton Gardiner, photographer

The Wolfsonian–Florida International
University
1001 Washington Ave
Miami Beach, Florida 33139
USA
www.wolfsonian.org

*The Birth of Rome: Five Visions for
the Eternal City* is made possible by
the Italian Consulate General Miami,
the Italian Cultural Institute New York,
the U.S. Consular Agency Genoa,
and the Wolfsoniana–Fondazione
Regionale per la Cultura e lo
Spettacolo, to mark the Year of Italian
Culture in the United States.

The Wolfsonian receives ongoing
support from John S. and James
L. Knight Foundation; State of
Florida, Department of State,
Division of Cultural Affairs and the
Florida Council on Arts and Culture;
Miami-Dade County Department
of Cultural Affairs and the Cultural
Affairs Council, the Miami-Dade
County Mayor and Board of County
Commissioners; and City of Miami
Beach, Cultural Affairs Program,
Cultural Arts Council.

Published by The Wolfsonian–Florida
International University, Miami
Beach.

(c) 2013 Florida International
University Board of Trustees

Printed and bound in the United
States of America by Shapco.
First edition.

ISSN 2330-8915

Library of Congress Cataloging-in-
Publication Data

Barisione, Silvia, author.
  The birth of Rome : five visions
for the Eternal City / author, Silvia
Barisione. -- First edition.
     pages cm
  "No.1 in a series of publications
focused on core themes in the
Wolfsonian's collection."
  Includes bibliographical references.
  ISBN 978-0-9677359-6-2 (alk.
paper)
1. Collective memory and city
planning--Italy--Rome. 2. Fascism
and architecture--Italy--Rome. 3.
Rome (Italy)--Buildings, structures,
etc. 4. Wolfsoniana (Museum) I.
Wolfsonian-Florida International
University. II. Title.
  NA9204.R7B37 2013
  711'.40945632--dc23

                                        2013035607

THE BIRTH OF ROME

FIVE VISIONS FOR THE ETERNAL CITY

Silvia Barisione

FIU | **The Wolfsonian**
FLORIDA INTERNATIONAL UNIVERSITY

Director's Preface
Cathy Leff

The Wolfsonian was founded in 1986 to exhibit, document, and preserve the Mitchell Wolfson, Jr. Collection of Decorative and Propaganda Arts, a vast assemblage of objects that includes furniture, paintings, books, prints, industrial and decorative art objects, and ephemera. In 1997 it became a division of Florida International University (FIU), when Mitchell Wolfson, Jr. donated his collection and museum facility to the university. Though the institution has evolved over the years, at least two things have remained constant: a commitment to research and publishing, and Italy.

The Birth of Rome inaugurates a series of publications focused on the Wolfsonian's extensive holdings of artifacts spanning from the height of the Industrial Revolution to the end of the Second World War. Emphasizing specific areas of the collection, many of which may not be known to our readership, each installment will follow our own continued discovery of the stories that shaped and defined this transformative era. The subject of this first publication in the series—modern architectural and urban planning projects that illustrate the alliance between art, design, and ideology in Italy under Benito Mussolini—provides a microcosm of themes embedded in the collection as a whole. In documenting certain of the defining challenges of modernity, from the consolidation of national identities to the integration of tradition with revolutionary change, *The Birth of Rome* reminds us that the things we make are never merely things, but also means of persuasion that influence culture in real, if not immediately noticeable, ways.

The Birth of Rome is made possible through the support of the Italian Consulate General Miami, the Italian Cultural Institute New York, and the U.S. Consular Agency Genoa, to mark the Year of Italian Culture in the United States. Elements of the publication also appeared in an exhibition of the same title. I wish to acknowledge those individuals and organizations that contributed to its achievement: Adolfo Barattolo, Riccardo Viale, Anna Maria Saiano, Marcello Cambi, Gucci, Mediterranean Shipping Company S.A., the Poltrona Frau Group, the Funding Arts Network, the Leon

Levy Foundation, Aprile SpA, and Ansaldo Energy Inc.

Much recognition is due to Gianni Franzone and Matteo Fochessati of the Wolfsoniana–Fondazione Regionale per la Cultura e lo Spettacolo for lending their extensive time and expertise to this endeavor. Opened in Genoa as a study center in 1993 and expanded into a museum in 2005, the Wolfsoniana holds a significant portion of the Italian materials collected by Mitchell Wolfson, Jr.—materials gifted by him to the Fondazione Regionale per la Cultura e lo Spettacolo in 2007. The institution continues to be a close partner in the advancement of our shared missions.

I am grateful to curator Silvia Barisione for her incisive examination of the Wolfsonian's Italian holdings. Her research and essay draw attention to the deeply consequential relationship between politics and aesthetics that everywhere influences civic life.

I thank assistant curator Matthew Abess, who served as the primary editor of this publication; assistant director for research and academic initiatives Jon Mogul for his editorial contributions; exhibitions manager Lisa Li for coordinating the publication process; art director Mylinh Trieu Nguyen for her thoughtful design; and exhibition designer Richard Miltner, whose insights into the subject have proved invaluable.

A project of this scope requires the involvement of the entire Wolfsonian staff, and I wish to acknowledge those colleagues whose direct participation has been vital to its success: David Almeida, Kimberly Bergen, Martha Betancourt, Cathy Byrd, Steve Forero-Paz, Lynton Gardiner, Nicolae Harsanyi, Francis X. Luca, Lea Nickless, Amy Silverman, and James Taylor.

As ever, we are indebted to the founding vision of Mitchell Wolfson, Jr., whose commitment to the collection and preservation of our recent past has provided a singular resource for the study and appreciation of modern visual and material culture. The materials that he has gathered over more than three decades witness and affirm the ongoing relationship between human production and lived experience, inviting us into dialogue with the myriad forces that continue to act upon our sense of the world.

The Birth of Rome:
Five Visions for the Eternal City
Silvia Barisione

Though more than fifteen centuries have passed since the decline and fall of the Roman Empire, the Eternal City remains a durable image of authority, allegiance, and ancient splendor. Its founding myths and tangible patrimony proved especially salient sources in the formation of the Italian state out of many dialects and regional differences. Even before its inception as a modern state with the success of the Risorgimento—the nineteenth-century movement to free the Italian peninsula from foreign rulers and create a unified nation—Italian patriots invoked Rome as a means by which to rally diverse peoples behind a common cause. "Rome or death!" proclaimed Giuseppe Garibaldi, military leader and heroic icon of the Risorgimento, who prepared the way for the defeat of papal and French forces in 1870 and the subsequent transfer of the capital from Florence to Rome the next year. It was under a modified banner of national resurgence that in 1922 Benito Mussolini staged his militarily insignificant though tremendously symbolic March on Rome, initiating more than two decades of Fascist rule that sought to remake Italy after the image of Roman grandeur.

The following essay examines five visions for the Eternal City that illustrate the persistence of Rome in Italian national consciousness during the interwar period, when the ancient capital served as a core principle of self-conception, a critical instrument of state mobilization, and the foremost source for official efforts to reclaim the peninsula's imperial past. Through the rise and collapse of what the Fascist government would declare the Third Rome—as exemplified by the redevelopment of the Augustean zone; the Foro Mussolini physical education complex; Virgilio Marchi's unrealized Futurist architecture; the new zone of the city planned for the 1942 *Esposizione Universale di Roma* (EUR); and the Italian pavilion at the 1939 New York World's Fair—the myth of the Eternal City endured.

I.   The Myth of Rome

Recognizing the potency of the newly established capital as an emblem of release from centuries of internal division and foreign domination, the leaders of the recently unified Kingdom of Italy initiated the process of reconfiguring Rome. The first master plan of the city, approved in 1883, urged "the putting of the new among the ancient, creating [new quarters] around the old nucleus . . . and introducing new arterial roads," such that the life of the city would tend "tenaciously and irresistibly toward the centers of ancient greatness."[1] Densely developed historic neighborhoods were demolished to make way for massive thoroughfares. Imposing edifices were built to house new government ministries. Major archaeological excavations, begun shortly after the liberation of the city with the clearing and restoration of the Colosseum, continued in earnest throughout the 1880s and 1890s.[2]

   With Mussolini's rise to power after the March on Rome, the myth of the Eternal City—promoted by Risorgimento statesmen on behalf of the idea of a unified and liberal Italian state—was transformed by the Fascist regime into a cult of *Romanitá* (Romaness). Carrying the promise of redemption under the sign of the ancient Roman fasces— the bundle of rods bound to an axe carried by Roman lictors as a marker of judicial authority and later adopted as the symbol of the Fascist party[3] [pl. XVIII]—Mussolini renewed efforts to renovate the capital. Identifying himself with the founder of the Roman Empire, who claimed in his *Res Gestae* to have found Rome a city of brick and left it a city of marble,[4] Mussolini declared in 1925: "In five years Rome must appear marvelous to all the peoples of the world, vast, ordered, powerful, as it was in the time of the first empire of Augustus."[5] Already, he had divided the city's "urgent problems into two categories, those relating to its necessities and those regarding its magnificence."[6] The drive to relieve urban density and improve traffic circulation was to be combined with an explicit political program reflecting the Duce's vision for a modern Rome rooted in its imperial past.

This new emphasis on Rome as an imperial capital notwithstanding, the Fascist handling of the reconfiguration of Rome resembled that of the pre-Fascist period. Architect Marcello Piacentini became the main interpreter of Mussolini's vision of imperial grandeur, asserting an approach of *sventramenti* (disembowelments) and *isolamenti* (isolations) of ancient Roman monuments from the various architectural accretions of time. The Rome of the Grand Tour—picturesque, colorful, chaotic, its abandoned ruins casually coexisting with vernacular architecture—was completely denied by the regime. The Ente Nazionale Industrie Turistiche (ENIT; National Agency of Touristic Industries), produced pamphlets and posters illustrating the Rome of Mussolini, with its efficient means of transportation—thanks to the modern tramway system sanctioned by the new Governatorato (the municipal government established by Mussolini), travelers could easily enjoy views of the city's ancient buildings, such as the Cestia pyramid [pl. I]—as well as its recently excavated monuments, such as Trajan's Market.[pl. II]

Piacentini had previously disparaged this approach to the renovation of Rome. As he explained in an essay of 1916, Rome was more a "picturesque" than a "grandiose" city. "To conserve a city," he continued, "it is not enough to 'save' its monuments and its beautiful palaces, by isolating them and creating around them an entirely new setting; it is also necessary to save the ancient setting (*ambiente*), with which they were so intimately connected."[7] But with his assumption of the role of leading figure in the commission for the new master plan of the capital—approved by Mussolini and the Governatorato in 1931—Piacentini embraced the strategies of disembowelment and isolation in the pursuit of the Duce's Rome.

As per the Duce's wishes, the 1931 plan delineated an extensive renovation of the Augustean zone centered on the mausoleum of the Emperor Augustus. Four great traffic lanes connecting the ancient city center to newer districts were to be inserted within the surrounding square and the mausoleum liberated from the added superstructure of a

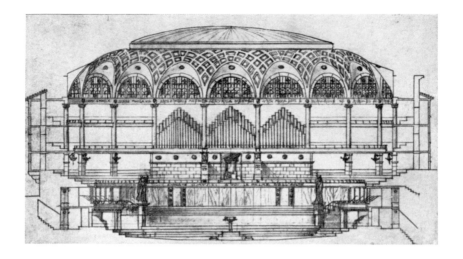

modern symphony hall, situated on top of the mausoleum and in active use since 1908.[8] Mussolini himself inaugurated the first stage of demolition in October 1934. From the rooftop of an adjacent building, pickaxe in hand, he declared that this ambitious project possessed "a triple utility: that of history and beauty, traffic, and hygiene."[9] Construction was scheduled for completion in 1937, the year of the Augustean bimillenary.

The 1931 plan was the culmination of years of attention to the mausoleum. A 1925 issue of the periodical *Capitolium* included a report on a proposed transformation of the mausoleum that had been commissioned to Piacentini by the City of Rome.[fig. 1] The proposal was aimed at preserving and improving the structure in its use as a symphony hall.[10] In 1927, the Federazione Fascista dell'Urbe (Fascist Federation of the City) presented a proposal by the architect Enrico Del Debbio [fig. 2] that sought "to isolate the monuments of ancient Rome, without altering their character through the construction of modern buildings."[11]

Within the overall scope of the plan for the redevelopment of the Augustean zone, restoration of the mausoleum held priority. Oversight duties were assigned to Antonio Muñoz, the Governatorato's principle consultant on Rome's architectonic heritage.[12] An expert on the restoration of medieval churches, Muñoz's recommendations were informed by the theories of Camillo Boito, according to

fig. 1 Renovation project for the Augusteo, 1925. Marcello Piacentini (1881–1960), architect

fig. 2 Augusteo as seen from Corso Umberto, 1927. Enrico Del Debbio (1891–1973), architect

whom historic buildings should be released of all elements extraneous to the original period, and then repaired rather than reconstructed. Instead of restoring the mausoleum to match its original condition, Muñoz transformed it into an authentic Roman ruin.[13] [fig. 3]

The final design of the piazza around the mausoleum was entrusted to architect Vittorio Morpurgo in 1934. The success of the recent rearrangement of the area surrounding the Mole Adriana (the mausoleum of the Emperor Hadrian, more commonly known as Castel Sant'Angelo) [fig. 4] heightened expectations for the Augustean project. Though Morpurgo admitted that the results of the excavation proved a relative disappointment, he nevertheless praised the intervention for making visible "a famous relic, buried without honor."[14] He further credited Mussolini for contributing to the design of the piazza, noting that the Duce was "always able to give his unmistakable imprint of Roman greatness to urban planning as to all other manifestations

of life."[15] Following Mussolini's orders, Morpurgo altered his initial proposal for the construction of a closed square in favor of a U shaped square facing the Tiber River, made possible by the demolition of a block of buildings on the riverfront boulevard.[fig. 5]

To enhance the piazza's identification with Augustus, Morpurgo suggested placing the recently excavated and restored Ara Pacis (the famous Altar of Augustan Peace) adjacent to the mausoleum. Housed in a rectangular

Giannino Marchig 19.?.34.

fig. 4 Drawing, View of the Mole Adriana, 1934. Giannino Marchig (1897–1983)

structure built of travertine, glass, and steel, the relocated altarpiece was celebrated alongside the mausoleum during the closing ceremonies for the emperor's bimillenary in September 1938.[16] Though the inauguration of the mausoleum did not stimulate the desired degree of fanfare—the public showcasing of the Ara Pacis, with its sculptural artwork dating from 9 BCE, received better reviews—critics commended the overall achievement. *Il Giornale d'Italia*, for instance, affirmed that the project succeeded in prompting the interaction of past and present, producing "not a contamination, but an eloquent demonstration of the eternal youth of the City."[17]

In addition to its extensive archaeological and architectural pursuits, the Fascist government commissioned mural paintings and decorations that advanced its image of Roman greatness. The creation of such works was deemed so crucial to the conveyance of Fascist political identity that in 1934 a law was proposed mandating that budgets for all public building projects allot at least two percent to commissioning painted or sculptural elements.[18] The embellishment of modern buildings in recently isolated sites would prove critical to the government's program of urban reconstruction, as contemporary works rooted in

fig. 5 View of the plastic model for the final approved rearrangement of the Augustean zone, 1936. Vittorio Morpurgo (1890–1966), architect

ancient idioms and classical iconography reinforced the eternal character of the capital.

The decorative centerpiece of the new Piazza Augusto Imperatore is Roman artist Ferruccio Ferrazzi's colossal mosaic, *Il Mito di Roma* (The Myth of Rome), designed at the invitation of Morpurgo for the façade of the National Institute for Social Security, a long porticoed building located at the northern end of the piazza.[fig. 6] In the periodical *L'Urbe*, Ferrazzi expressed his delight at the 1938 invitation,[19] noting that he was "fascinated by the idea of a fabulous narration . . . of a *fantastic Roman reality*." In a style that he defined as "*new mythic naturalism*," he set out to tell a story that the entire populous would know and understand—art, he contended, "must go back to the street [as an] expression of the people and for the people."[20] [fig. 7]

In addition to his selected subject—the founding myth of the Eternal City—Ferrazzi's decision to realize the work as a mosaic emphasized the inextricable bond between the modern buildings at the perimeter of the piazza and the ancient monument at its center. A 1941 article appearing in *Stile* applauded architecture for abandoning mere plastic decoration in favor of expressing a thought, which, "on the exterior walls, cannot be told through the fresco, but

fig. 6 Detail of the plastic model showing *Il Mito di Roma* (The Myth of Rome) on the façade of the National Institute for Social Security, 1936. Vittorio Morpurgo (1890–1966), architect

through the glass mosaic, which lasts eternally." The article went on to argue that, more than simply an Italian tradition, the mosaic technique should be understood as authentically Roman.[21]

Ferrazzi's own pictorial research never abandoned the analytical study of the art of the ancient past. His mosaic and encaustic painting was influenced by related findings in the excavation of Pompeii. In 1927, he was commissioned to create the frescoes and mosaics for the mausoleum in the Villa Ottolenghi [pl. VIII] at Acqui Terme, designed by Piacentini.[22] Dealing with the subject of the apocalypse, Ferrazzi realized these frescoes in the postwar years, incorporating the figure of Aurora already present in his design for *Il Mito di Roma*.[23] [figs. 8–9]

The studies for the mosaic in the Piazza Augusto Imperatore—of which the centerpiece and one of the six surrounding panels are in The Wolfsonian's permanent collection—document the elaboration of the work from the general planning of the triptych, rising three floors in height above the balcony on the building's façade, to the final scale template. The humble origins (*exiguis initiis*) of Rome, as signified by the Latin inscription[24] above the opening of the balcony doorway,[pl. X] are told through the image of the mythical twin brothers, Romulus and Remus, who are said to have been nurtured by a she-wolf after being left to die in a basket on the Tiber River.

fig. 7 Photograph of Ferruccio Ferrazzi with his cartoon for *Tevere* (Tiber), from *Il Mito di Roma* (The Myth of Rome), 1940

The first study for the central panel personifies the Tiber as a nude young man, departing from the tradition of depicting the river as an elder. With the twins in his arms and the she-wolf below him, the figure stands in a dark green setting that in the subsequent two studies transitions into warm pink tones, referring to the rise of Aurora, presented as an androgynous woman floating among her horses in a whirl of clouds.[pl. XIV-XV] The architectural drawing of the façade shows the mosaic in situ, with the landscape rendered as an abstract composition of yellow stripes on a green ground.[pl. IX] The outlined perspective view of the final drawings clarifies this element as fields of

fig. 8 Photograph of Ferruccio Ferrazzi's daughters with his cartoon for *Aurora*, from *Il Mito di Roma* (The Myth of Rome), 1940

grain stretching upwards from the muddy grey line of the Tiber River to the thin blue contour of the sea in Ostia.[pl. XI]

Six pagan divinities, three on each side, watching over the central scene, complete the triptych.[pl. XVI] Their presence serves as a prelude to the future splendor of Rome, while the cultivated land in the background references the recently reclaimed marshland of the Agro Romano, carried out under the direction of the Fascist regime.[25] The divinities thus bring their ancient, mythic character to bear on the young capital, making a "fantastic Roman reality" of the modern Eternal City.

17

fig. 9 Photograph showing *L'Aurora* and *La Nascita* (The Birth), from Ferruccio Ferrazzi's cycle of frescoes in the mausoleum of the Villa Ottolenghi at Acqui Terme, 1953–57

II.   Ancient Modern Rome

On the other side of the Tiber, set on the slopes of the
Monte Mario, is the Foro Mussolini, the first major architectural and urban planning project initiated under the
Fascist regime.[pl. XVIII] Renato Ricci, president of the Opera
Nazionale Balilla (ONB), commissioned the complex to
Enrico Del Debbio in 1927. The ONB had been founded
one year earlier with the purpose of presiding over the
spiritual, physical, and military education of Italian youth
from eight to eighteen years of age.[26] Leading the national
campaign for physical education, Ricci traveled through

fig. 10 Photograph of the Foro Mussolini under construction, 1932. Romolo Del Papa, photographer

the United Kingdom and the United States to study foreign equivalents of the youth organization and its intended facilities. Upon its completion, Piacentini praised the Foro as a true "city of physical education," an "ancient modernized Gymnasium."[27] Inspired by the Roman forums of the Imperial Age, Del Debbio designed within the context of the classical tradition. While the architect selected the refined white marble of the Apuane Alps for most of the construction rather than the warm tonality of Roman travertine, the Fascist Academy of Physical Education was colored Pompeian red. The repetition of the "broken tympanum" above the windows of the Academy echoes the work of Novecento architects in Milan, who, for their part, reinterpreted the *neo*classical traditions of their city.[fig. 10]

The Foro complex is host to a marble stadium surrounded by sixty monumental statues. Each standing four meters high, their virile and muscular bodies testify to the Fascist program of improving the health and strength of the nation through physical activity, as reflected in the Roman-derived sculptural proportions. Each Italian province contributed a statue representing a sport, often selected for its association with the particular city of provenance.

On behalf of Venice, the sculptor Eugenio Baroni submitted a bronze maquette of a man sailing [pl. XXIII] in a form that would be faithfully reproduced in the full scale marble statue. Aldo Buttini's maquette of a boy holding a scroll [pl. XXIV] features fine, elongated lines that became heavy and vigorous in the realized statue installed in one of the niches of the Academy building. A monumental statue of a Balilla, [pl. XXVI] designed by Aroldo Bellini and inaugurated in 1936 to celebrate the tenth anniversary of the ONB, wears the uniform of the Fascist youth organization and holds a rifle on his

fig. 11 Marble stadium, Foro Mussolini, 1943. Sepp Schüller, photographer

shoulder, signaling the physical capacity and military skill of the nation in its entirety. [pl. XXV]

If the Balilla and marble athletes came to be symbols of the Foro,[fig. 11-13] the gigantic Mussolini obelisk [pl. XXVIII] was its de facto logo, widely reproduced on medals, posters, and brochures.[pl. XXIX-XXXI] Gifted to the Duce by a group of industrialists from Carrara, it was designed by the architect Costantino Costantini, who also took part in the design of the tennis stadium. Finding a suitably large piece of marble in the Carrara quarry was no simple task. The stone's discovery, fabrication, transport, and raising were covered in leading propaganda publications, where it was contextualized as part of an ongoing narrative beginning in 1928 and concluding with its final installation [fig. 14] on the first day of the tenth year of the Fascist revolution (October 28, 1932). The marble was described as having been "cut with male confidence"[28] and "the whole undertaking" celebrated as a "real triumph of the modern Italian technic"[29]—a repertoire of knowledge and skills inherited directly from the Romans, as the central presidium of the ONB proudly pointed out.[30]

III.   Futurist Rome

While on one side Fascism stood as the embodiment of Roman authority and martial skill, artists, writers, and designers of the Futurist movement argued that the world had changed irrevocably as a result of modern technology and that Fascism should be understood as the natural political outcome of new thinking initiated by these changes.[31] Even so, invocations of the Roman past figured in the work of some Futurists.

Following the deaths of pioneering Futurists Umberto Boccioni and Antonio Sant'Elia in the First World War, Filippo Tommaso Marinetti, founder and prime mover of the Futurist movement, engaged new members in reviving its revolutionary aesthetic program. Among them was the young architect Virgilio Marchi, who moved from Livorno to Rome in 1920 and joined the Roman Futurist group led by Giacomo Balla. In the same year, he published his *Manifesto dell'architettura futurista* in the journal *Roma Futurista*. The polemic opens with a denouncement of leading trends in contemporary architecture as merely the "fruit of a remixing of traditional prototypes and vulgar speculation," going on to proclaim: "It is necessary to abandon the static verticality and horizontality of standard construction and seek plastic movement through the dynamic impulse of curves, of planes of revolution, of force lines."[32] Influenced by Sant'Elia's architectural drawings, Marchi elaborated

fig. 14 The raising of the monolith of Carrara, Foro Mussolini, 1932. Axel von Graefe (1900–), photographer

fantastic visions of the built environment without—according to architectural historian Dennis Doordan—reconciling the two dimensions of his vision: the lyrical and the practical. Nor did he see any of his renderings realized.

Marchi's 1931 book *Italia Nuova Architettura Nuova* includes a series of drawings for Futurist building projects.[33] Among them, *La città di cemento* (The City of Cement)[pl. XXXII] illustrates a multilevel building complex composed of oblique lines and aerodynamic surfaces. This visionary cityscape is a prelude to Marchi's later projects for a new transportation system in Rome, such as *Testata di Ponte* (Bridgehead),[pl. XXXIII] illustrated in the unpublished book *I vertici azzurri di Roma (Il futuro di Roma)* addressing contemporary debates on the urban development of the capital.[34] The vibrant curves of *La città di cemento* harden in these later works, including his representations of the bridge over the river Aniene, once the primary water supply for many Roman aqueducts: pillars appear as stylized fasces and arches are peaked by Roman eagles,[pl. XXXIV] asserting the eternal bond of the Fascist capital with its ancient architectonic source.

The Universal Exposition of Rome

The *Esposizione Universale di Roma* (EUR) was the most ambitious of the Fascist building programs carried out in the course of the expansion of the Eternal City. Intended as a fairground for the celebration of the twentieth anniversary of the Fascist Revolution and the fifth anniversary of Mussolini's Empire, declared in 1936 after the Italian conquest of Ethiopia, the permanent buildings and future pavilions were characterized by their architects' efforts to reach suitable compromises between competing ideas about modern Italy and its built environment. As architectural historian Richard Etlin has remarked of the project:

"Modernity and monumentality, rationalism and classicism were to be fused together in the service of an imperial vision of the Fascist state."[35] While the world's fairs of the past decade had presented A Century of Progress (Chicago, 1933–34), Art and Technology in Modern Life (Paris, 1937), and The World of Tomorrow (New York, 1939–40), the *Olimpiadi della Civiltà* (Olympics of Civilization; Rome, 1942) would pay tribute to the worldwide cultural influence of Roman civilization.

Marcello Piacentini, commissioned to develop the master plan, assembled a team of Rationalist architects whose first proposal was approved by Mussolini in 1937.[36] The Palazzo della Civiltà Italiana, the most prominent and iconic of the new buildings in the EUR, is emblematic of the aesthetic middle ground of Fascist architecture as it developed in the 1930s.[pl. XXXVII–XXXIX] Designed by architects Ernesto Bruno Lapadula, Giovanni Guerrini, and Mario Romano, the so-called Square Colosseum integrates the modernist principles of Rationalism with Roman precedents to articulate the greatness of Italian civilization now as then, expressing its Romaness in six floors of symmetrical travertine arcades decorated by classical statues and inscriptions. The nearby Palazzo dei Congressi, designed by the Rationalist architect Adalberto Libera, perfects this compromise between past and present in its joining of a columnar front porch with a dome, referencing both the Pantheon in Rome and early Christian basilicas.[fig. 15, bottom right]

fig. 16 Medal, *Roma Aeterna – Esposizione Universale Roma, 1942-XX* (Eternal Rome – Universal Exposition Rome, 1942-Year Twenty of the Fascist Revolution), c. 1939

In 1939, a competition was announced for a never-realized mosaic decoration of the main hall of the Palazzo dei Congressi addressing a set of themes related to the history of Rome: *The Beginnings of Rome, The Empire, Renaissance and Universality of the Church,* and *Mussolini's Rome.* As prescribed by the competition guidelines, Alberto Salietti's submissions illustrated parades of figures in architectural settings representing significant periods in the development of Rome: the temple of Capitoline Jove for the beginnings of Rome, the Arch of Constantine for the Empire, St. Peter's Basilica for the Renaissance and the Church, and, for Fascist Rome, the EUR under construction.[pl. XL–XLIII] In this last study, Salietti juxtaposed ancient and modern by placing the Colosseum in line with the Palazzo della Civiltà Italiana, with both watched over by the planned colossal arch designed by Adalberto Libera. Although the arch was never realized, this engineering masterpiece became the visionary symbol of the audacious technological outlook of the exhibition. It was reproduced on the official EUR medal as a modern counterpart to the image of the goddess Rome (modeled after that used on ancient Roman coinage) reproduced on the other side of the medal,[fig. 16] as well as on an official poster[pl. XXXV] designed by Giorgio Quaroni. (Quaroni was also one of the artists who won the competition for the mosaic of the Palazzo dei Congressi, together with Giovanni Guerrini, Achille Capizzano, and Franco Gentilini.)

The EUR never took place owing to the Second World War. The development of the district was completed following the end of the conflict, and the EUR is now a neighborhood in the southern sector of the Eternal City. Its severe architectural monuments from the interwar period stand as a reminder of the Olympics of Civilization envisioned by the planners and architects of Mussolini's Rome.

V. Rome at the World of Tomorrow

Vastly popular world's fairs and expositions provided Italian architects, artists, and designers a platform for displaying the key positions around which they developed representations of the nation. If Italian modernity at the Century of Progress fair (Chicago, 1933–34) was embodied by the Rationalist pavilion of architects Mario De Renzi and Adalberto Libera,[fig. 17] emblazoned at its entrance with a colossal stylized fasces, the Italian pavilion at the World of Tomorrow fair (New York, 1939) served as a clear expression of the return to order that characterized the final years of the Third Rome. Designed by the architect Michele Busiri Vici, it was described in the fair's official guide book as "an ingenuous synthesis of the architecture of classical Rome and modern Italy."37 [pl. XLV–XLIX]

Two symmetrical colonnades defined the forecourt of the 1939 pavilion, leading to its main structure topped by a tower. Each side of the tower was decorated with thin stylized fasces, its top serving as a base for a replica of the statue of the goddess Rome from the Capitoline Hill. A cascade of water descended from this pedestal, splashing down the façade into a pool; at night, it presented a "thrilling spectacle" thanks to the use of vitreous paste and an unusual underwater lighting system, according to an

fig. 17 View of the Italian Pavilion at the 1933 Chicago World's Fair. C. R. Childs Company, Chicago, photographer

fig. 18 Photograph of the Restaurant Conte di Savoia inside the Italian Pavilion at the 1939 New York World's Fair.

advertisement in the March 5, 1939, issue of the *New York Times*.[38] The periodical *Casabella* pronounced the structure a "paradoxical pavilion" for its layered quotations from classical architecture,[39] though nevertheless urged visiting the exhibitions inside, which *Architectural Forum* called "some of the most gaily designed exhibits in the Fair," even as it derided the pavilion architecture as "a curious perversion of classical precedent."[40] Lapadula, one of the architects responsible for designing the Palazzo della Civiltà Italiana for the EUR, compared the white and blue of the pavilion to a "house in Capri,"[41] suggesting an attempt to connect the structure to recent trends in Rationalist architecture—its practitioners claimed to take inspiration from the flat roofs and smooth surfaces that characterize the vernacular architecture of the Mediterranean coast (Capri, Ischia, and the Amalfi Coast, especially) in their development of a modern Italian idiom—despite the inclusion of decorative and formal elements that Rationalist architects wholly rejected.

While most of the pavilions at the World of Tomorrow showcased technological advances and commercial wares—and the Italian displays were no exception—civilization served as the core theme of the Italian pavilion. Its exhibition of contemporary Italian painting and sculpture, which featured works drawn from the National and Municipal Galleries of Rome, Florence, Milan, and Turin, offered a general outline of the development of Italian fine arts from the advent to the present of Fascist Italy. The exhibition catalogue paid tribute to the selection of works on display, arguing that, "after the confusion of the post-war years, Italian art detached itself from artistic internationalism, so fashionable at that time, and sought its greatness in a return to the famous masters of the past: without copying them, it tried to absorb their fundamental spirit."[42] Sculptor Antonio Berti's portrait of Paola Ojetti [pl. LI] reflects the formal purity and classicism advocated by the subject's father, Ugo Ojetti, an art critic, journalist, and one of the most influential figures in the evolution of official Fascist culture; the static pose of the bronze bust evokes both Roman and Renaissance statuary. Adolfo Wildt's sculpture of journalist Nicola Bonservizi [pl. LII] in a Novecento style, at once symbolist and visionary, further reflects the return to order of late-1930s Italian cultural production.

As the works of art on display mirrored the classical lines of the pavilion architecture, so did the interiors seen in Busiri Vici's architectural drawings. The stained glass window at the entrance, designed by Assia Busiri Vici, is emblematic of the general approach to the pavilion interiors in its depiction of a metaphysical landscape replete with Roman references.[pl. L] *Architectural Forum* made no mention of the window, though it did recommend visiting "the lush restaurant and bar" on the second floor, which architect Gustavo Pulitzer adapted from his design for the restaurant of the SS *Conte di Savoia*.[fig. 18] The famous ocean liner was renowned for the clean lines of Pulitzer's interiors, distinguished by the abandonment of historic styles and harmonization with, rather than disavowal of, the naval structure of the ship. Here, modernity prevailed over historicist reconstructions of the past, spreading across the Atlantic an internationalist expression of interwar Italian identity.

1   "Premessa e caratteri generali," in "Urbanistica della Roma Mussoliniana," special issue, *Architettura* (1936): 15–16.

2   Joshua Arthurs, *Excavating Modernity: The Roman Past in Fascist Italy* (Ithaca and London: Cornell University Press, 2012), 14.

3   Hence the term *fascismo*. See Robert Hughes, *Rome: A Cultural, Visual, and Personal History* (New York: Alfred A. Knopf, 2011), 407. Hughes also notes that it was the poet Gabriele D'Annunzio "who first made popular the Roman salutes, the black shirts, the speeches from the balcony, the marches and the 'oceanic' demonstrations that we associate primarily with the Duce—a title, not incidentally, that the poet wanted to reserve for himself," ibid., 389.

4   Arthurs, 66.

5   Benito Mussolini, in *Opera Omnia*, ed. Edoardo Susmel and Duilo Susmel (Florence: La Fenice, 1951), 22:47, quoted in Arthurs, 66.

6   "Premessa e caratteri generali," 16.

7   Marcello Piacentini, *Sulla conservazione della bellezza di Roma e sullo sviluppo della città moderna* (Rome, 1916), 7–9, quoted in Richard A. Etlin, "Nationalism in Modern Italian Architecture, 1890–1940," in *Nationalism in the Visual Arts,* ed. Richard A. Etlin (Washington, DC: National Gallery of Art, 1991), 92.

8   The engineer Edmondo Sanjust included provisions for the excavation of the mausoleum in his master plan of 1909. Though the plan was approved, and with it Sanjust's proposal for separating the mausoleum from the surrounding symphony hall without altering the overall aspect of the structure, it was not carried out owing to rapid population growth and the eventual outbreak of the First World War.

9   Mussolini, in *Opera Omnia* 26:367–68, quoted in Arthurs, 69.

10 "La trasformazione dell'Augusteo," *Capitolium* 1, no. 1 (1925): 24–27.

11 *La sistemazione della zona Augustea* (Rome: Federazione Fascista dell'Urbe, 1927), 3.

12 Muñoz, a member of the commission for the city's master plan, was superintendent of the monuments in Lazio from 1914 to 1928, and was later named head of the Department of Antiquities and Fine Arts of the Governatorato. He founded the periodical *L'Urbe* in 1936.

13 See Spiro Kostof, "The Emperor and the Duce: The Planning of Piazzale Augusto Imperatore in Rome," in *Art and Architecture in the Service of Politics*, ed. Henry A. Millon and Linda Nochlin (Cambridge, MA: MIT Press, 1978), 289.

14 Vittorio Morpurgo, "La sistemazione augustea," *Capitolium* 12, no. 3 (1937): 146.

15 Ibid., 149.

16 In 2006 Morpurgo's shrine for the Ara Pacis was replaced by a controversial building designed by American architect Richard Meier.

17 Alessandro Bacchiani, "L'ara augustea della pace vittoriosa domini nella Roma imperiale di oggi," *Il Giornale d'Italia*, March 4, 1937, quoted in Arthurs, 72–73.

18 The proposal, which sparked heated debate in the journals of the time, was advocated by Giuseppe Bottai, who was appointed as Minister of National Education in 1936. The initiative only became law in 1942.

19 The official letter of commission to Ferrazzi from the Istituto Nazionale Fascista della Previdenza Sociale is dated June 1939. It is documented in the Ferrazzi Archive, Rome.

20 Antonio Muñoz, "Il Mito di Roma: musaico di Ferruccio Ferrazzi nella piazza d'Augusto Imperatore," *L'Urbe* 6, no. 5 (1941): 28–30. Italics in the original.

21 "Mosaici nell'architettura," special issue, *Lo stile nella casa e nell'arredamento*, nos. 5–6 (1941): 101–102.

22 The Wolfsonian's collection includes the plaster model of the mausoleum, designed by Piacentini in collaboration with Ernesto Rapisardi. As the model shows, the general plan called for the construction of a perimeter arcade in the villa's park. Ferrazzi's work for the mausoleum is documented in Flaminio Gualdoni, "Ferrazzi e gli Ottolenghi," in *Le capitali d'Italia Torino Roma, 1911–1946, arti produzione spettacolo*, ed. Marisa Vescovo and Netta Vespignani (Milan: Electa Mondadori, 1997), 45–48, ill. 203–14.

23 Ferrazzi developed the same motif of Aurora in his 1941 encaustic painting for Palazzo Bo, University of Padua. See the study in *Muri ai pittori. Pittura murale e decorazione in Italia, 1930–1950*, ed. Vittorio Fagone, Giovanna Ginex, and Tulliola Sparagni (Milan: Mazzotta, 1999), 165, fig. 52.

24 The inscription, "His Ab Exiguis Profecta Initiis Roma," is taken from Livy's preface to *Ab Urbe Condita*.

25 Ferrazzi selected this same subject for his mosaic of the *Annunciation* on the facade of the church of Sabaudia, a new town in the Agro Pontino—an area of reclaimed marshland outside of Rome—founded in 1934.

26 The name Balilla derives from the story of a young Genoese boy who in 1746 threw a stone at an Austrian soldier, setting off a popular revolt against the Austrians. The tale was referenced as an instance of courage and strength from which the young Fascist generation could take inspiration.

27 Marcello Piacentini, "Il Foro Mussolini in Roma – arch. Enrico Del Debbio," *Architettura* 11–12 (1933): 65.

28 Giacomo di Castelnuovo, "Roma di Mussolini: primo decennale della Rivoluzione Fascista," in "Roma di Mussolini – Decennale," special issue, *Opere Pubbliche* 2, no. 10 (1932): 362.

29 Ibid., 365.

30 *L'Obelisco Mussolini* (Rome: Edizione a cura della Presidenza Centrale dell'Opera Balilla, 1934).

31 The founder of the Futurist movement, Filippo Tommaso Marinetti, supported Mussolini's rise to power and influenced his revolutionary aesthetic program during the early years of Fascism.

32 Virgilio Marchi, "Manifesto dell'architettura futurista," *Roma Futurista*, February 29, 1920, quoted in Dennis P. Doordan, *Building Modern Italy: Italian Architecture, 1914–1936* (New York: Princeton Architectural Press, 1988), 19.

33 The three drawings in the Wolfsonian's collection are published in Virgilio Marchi, *Italia Nuova Architettura Nuova* (Rome and Foligno: Franco Campitelli Editore, 1931). TD1989.65.5 appears, slightly modified, under the main title heading; TD1989.65.1 with the title *Scorcio di città* (Glimpse of the City), 82, fig. 20; and TD1989.65.2 with the title *Cavalcavia sull'Aniene* (Aniene Overpass), 216, fig. 45.

34 *Testata di ponte* is illustrated in the layout of the book by the publisher Franco Campitelli, dated 1926. See Ezio Godoli and Milva Giacomelli, ed., *Virgilio Marchi. Scritti di architettura*, vol. 1, *Architettura futurista. I vertici azzurri di Roma (Il futuro di Roma)* (Florence: Octavo Franco Cantini, 1995), 153.

35 Richard A. Etlin, *Modernism in Italian Architecture, 1890–1940* (Cambridge and London: MIT Press, 1991), 491.

36 See "Il piano regolatore dell'Esposizione Universale di Roma, 1941–1942," *Casabella* 10, no. 114 (1937): 4–15.

37 *Official Guide Book. New York World's Fair 1939* (New York: Exposition Publications, Inc., 1939), 105.

38 "Italy at the World's Fair," advertisement, *New York Times*, sec. 8, March 5,1939, 64.

39 "Cronaca della Esposizione Universale di New York," *Casabella* 11, no. 141 (1939): 22–23.

40 "Italy," *Architectural Forum* 70, no. 6 (1939): 456.

41 Bruno Lapadula, "Visita alla Fiera Mondiale di Nuova York 1939," *Architettura* 18, no. 7 (1939): 396.

42 *Mostra d'Arte Contemporanea Italiana – Padiglione Italiano all'Esposizione Universale di New York MCMXXXIX* (Milan: Editoriale Domus S.A.: 1939), 35. The marble version of Adolfo Wildt's sculpture of Nicola Bonservizi from the Modern Art Gallery, Milan, is published on p. 55; Antonio Berti's bronze copy of his bust of Paola Ojetti from the Civic Museum, Turin, on p. 94.

PLATES

I.
Poster, *Tramvie del Governatorato* (Tramways of the Governorate), 1927.
Ente Nazionale Industrie Turistiche (ENIT), publisher. Barabino & Graeve,
Genoa, printer

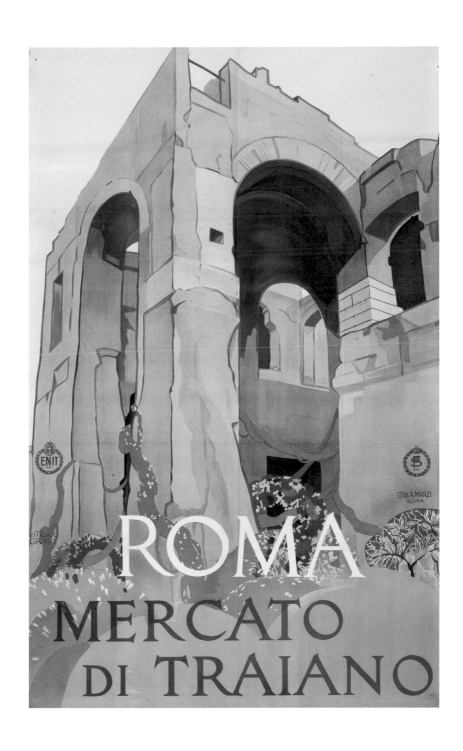

II.
Poster, *Roma. Mercato di Traiano* (Rome. Trajan's Market), c. 1930. Vittorio Grassi (1878–1958), designer. Ente Nazionale Industrie Turistiche (ENIT), publisher. A. Marzi, Rome, printer

III.
Poster, *Alle Wege führen nach Rom* (All Roads Lead to Rome), 1937. Severo (Sepo) Pozzati (1895–1983), designer. Ente Nazionale Industrie Turistiche (ENIT), publisher. Coen & Co., Milan, printer

IV.
Poster, *3 Ore Funivia Aquila Gran Sasso* (3 Hour Cableway Aquila Gran Sasso), 1934 (designed 1932). Umberto Noni, designer. Barabino & Graeve, Genoa, printer

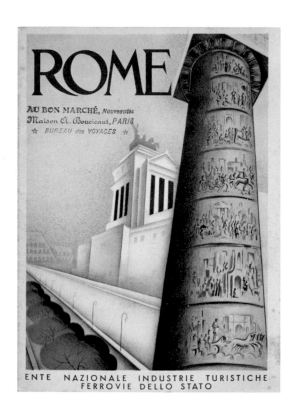

V.
Pamphlet cover, *Rome*, 1933.
Ente Nazionale Industrie
Turistiche (ENIT), publisher

VI.
Pamphlet cover, *Rome*, 1936.
Ente Nazionale Industrie
Turistiche (ENIT), publisher

VII.
Poster, *Roma*, c. 1939. Ente Nazionale Industrie Turistiche (ENIT), publisher.
Pizzi & Pizio, Milan and Rome, printer

VIII.
Model, Layout of the mausoleum in the Villa Ottolenghi at Acqui Terme, c. 1930.
Marcello Piacentini (1881–1960), architect

IX.
Study for *Il Mito di Roma* (The Myth of Rome) with detail of building façade, 1940.
Ferruccio Ferrazzi (1891–1978), artist. Vittorio Morpurgo (1890–1966), architect

43

(Left) **X.**
Study for *Il Mito di Roma*
(The Myth of Rome)
with detail of balcony,
1940. Ferruccio Ferrazzi
(1891–1978)

(Right) **XI.**
Cartoon, *Tevere* (Tiber),
from *Il Mito di Roma*
(The Myth of Rome),
1940. Ferruccio Ferrazzi
(1891–1978)

44

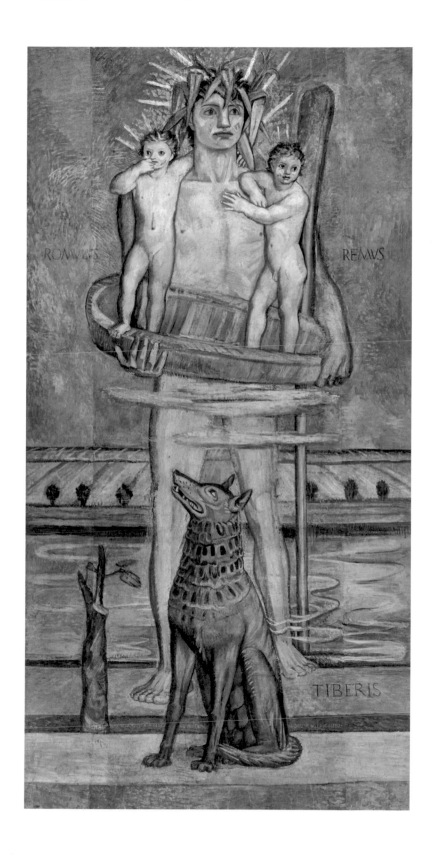

XII.
Detail of Tiber, Romulus, and Remus,
from the mosaic *Il Mito di Roma*
(The Myth of Rome) by Ferruccio
Ferrazzi, 1940

46

XIII.
Detail of the she-wolf, from the
mosaic *Il Mito di Roma* (The Myth of
Rome) by Ferruccio Ferrazzi, 1940

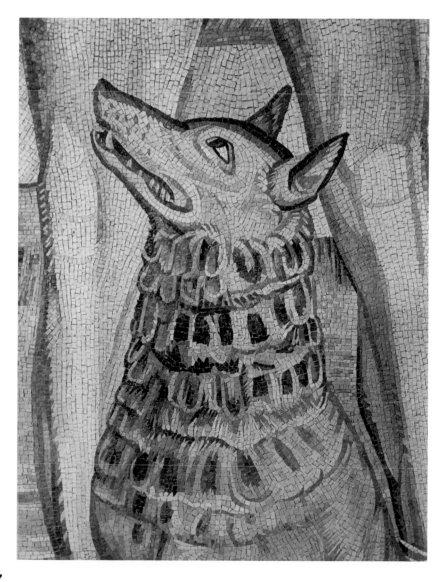

(Top) **XIV.**
Cartoon, *Aurora*, from *Il Mito di Roma*
(The Myth of Rome), 1940. Ferruccio
Ferrazzi (1891–1978)

(Bottom) **XV.**
Detail of *Aurora*, from the mosaic *Il
Mito di Roma* (The Myth of Rome) by
Ferruccio Ferrazzi, 1940

XVI.
Cartoon, *Vesta*, from *Il Mito di Roma* (The Myth of Rome), 1940.
Ferruccio Ferrazzi (1891–1978)

XVII.
Viewbook, *Il Foro Mussolini*, c. 1937. E. Verdesi, Rome, publisher

FORO MVSSOLINI - VEDVTA D'ASSIEME·

XVIII.
Overview of the Foro Mussolini, from *Progetti di costruzioni* (Construction Projects),
1928. Enrico Del Debbio (1891–1973), architect

51

(Top) **XIX.**
Photograph of the Foro Mussolini under construction, 1932. Romolo Del Papa, photographer

(Bottom) **XX.**
Photograph of the Foro Mussolini under construction, 1932. Romolo Del Papa, photographer

(Top) **XXI.**
Photograph of the Foro Mussolini under
construction, 1932. Romolo Del Papa,
photographer

(Bottom) **XXII.**
Photograph showing the raising of the
monolith of Carrara, Foro Mussolini,
1932. Romolo Del Papa, photographer

53

XXIII.
Maquette, *La vela* (The Sail), c. 1933. For a statue in the Foro Mussolini, Rome.
Eugenio Baroni (1880–1935)

XXIV.
Maquette, *Fanciullo con cartiglio* (Young Boy with Scroll), c. 1933. For a statue in the
Foro Mussolini, Rome. Aldo Buttini (1898–1957)

XXV.
Poster, *1a leva artistica della G. I. L.* (First Art Benefit for the G. I. L.), c. 1942.
Filippo Romoli (1901–1969), designer. SAIGA, formerly Barabino & Graeve,
Genoa, printer

XXVI.
Photograph showing statue of the Balilla, Foro Mussolini, c. 1937.
George Hoyningen-Huene (1900–1968), photographer

XXVII.
Photograph of the marble stadium, Foro Mussolini, c. 1937.
George Hoyningen-Huene (1900–1968), photographer

58

XXVIII.
Photograph showing the monolith of Carrara, Foro Mussolini, c. 1937.
George Hoyningen-Huene (1900–1968), photographer

59

XXIX.
Poster, *Settimana del Balilla, 5–10 Dicembre XIV, Genova* (Balilla Youth Movement Week, December 5–10, Year Fourteen of the Fascist Revolution, Genoa), 1935. C. M., designer. Barabino & Graeve, Genoa, printer

XXXII.
Perspective study, *La Città di Cemento* (The Concrete City), c. 1919. Virgilio Marchi (1895–1960). Stabilimento per la Riproduzione Disegni L. Bazzichelli, Rome, printer

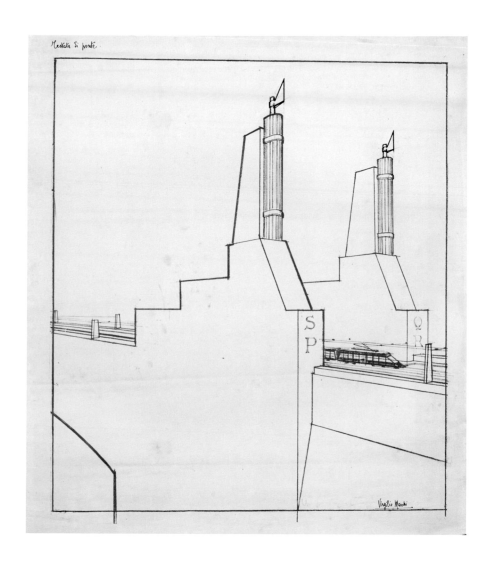

XXXIII.
Perspective study, *Testata di ponte* (Bridgehead), 1926. Virgilio Marchi
(1895–1960)

XXXIV.
Perspective study, *Progetto di grande tramvia elettrica di cintura a Roma* (Project for Big Electrical Tramway around Rome), c. 1927. Virgilio Marchi (1895–1960)

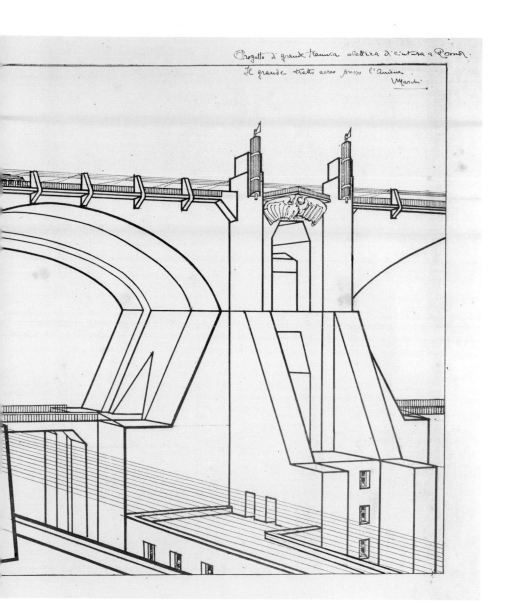

Progetto d'grande tramvia elettrica d'cintura a Roma.
Il grande tratto aereo presso l'Aniene.
Marchi

65

XXXV.
Poster, *Roma 1942 XX. Esposizione Universale* (Rome 1942 Year Twenty of the Fascist Revolution. Universal Exposition), 1939. Giorgio Quaroni (1907–1960), designer. Edizioni dell'Esposizione Universale, Rome, publisher. SAIGA, formerly Barabino & Graeve, Genoa, printer

XXXVI.
Poster, *E.42. Esposizione Universale di Roma. Planimetria Generale* (E.42. Universal Exposition of Rome. General Masterplan), 1939. Edizioni dell'Esposizione Universale, Rome, publisher

XXXVII.
Elevation sketch
of the Palazzo della
Cività Italiana,
c. 1937. Giovanni
Guerrini (1887–
1972)

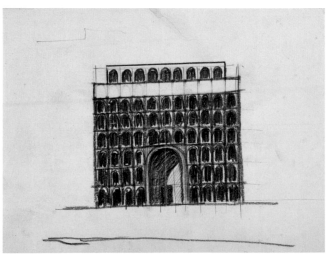

XXXVIII.
Elevation sketch
of the Palazzo della
Cività Italiana,
c. 1937. Giovanni
Guerrini (1887–
1972)

XXXIX.
Plan sketch of the Palazzo della Civiltà Italiana, c. 1937.
Giovanni Guerrini (1887–1972)

XL.
Study, *Le Origini di Roma* (The Beginnings of Rome), 1940–41. For the competition
"Mosaic Decoration in the Hall of the Palazzo dei Congressi," E42, Rome. Alberto
Salietti (1892–1961)

XLI.
Study, *L'Impero* (The Empire), 1940–41. For the competition "Mosaic Decoration
in the Hall of the Palazzo dei Congressi," E42, Rome. Alberto Salietti (1892–1961)

XLII.
Study, *Rinascimento e Universalità della Chiesa* (Renaissance and Universality of the Church), 1940–41. For the competition "Mosaic Decoration in the Hall of the Palazzo dei Congressi," E42, Rome. Alberto Salietti (1892–1961)

XLIII.
Study, *Roma di Mussolini* (Mussolini's Rome), 1940–41. For the competition
"Mosaic Decoration in the Hall of the Palazzo dei Congressi," E42, Rome.
Alberto Salietti (1892–1961)

XLIV.
Periodical advertisement, from *New York Times*, sec. 8, May 5, 1939.

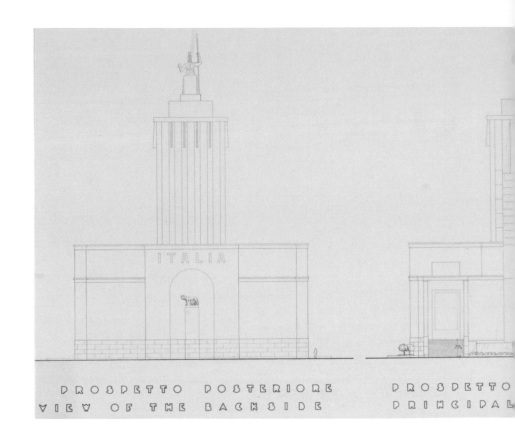

PROSPETTO POSTERIORE   PROSPETTO
VIEW OF THE BACKSIDE   PRINCIPAL

XLV.
Elevations and section, *Italian Pavilion New York World's Fair 1939: View of the Backside, Principal View, Cross Section*, 1938. Michele Busiri Vici (1894–1981)

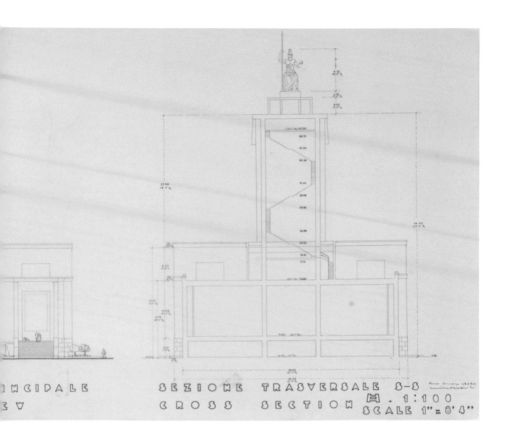

INGIPALE   SEZIONE TRASVERSALE S-S
  A   CROSS   SECTION   . 1:100
                                        SCALE 1" = 8' 4"

XLVI.
Model of the Italian Pavilion, New York World's Fair, 1939. Michele Busiri Vici
(1894–1981), architect

82

XLVII.
View of the Italian Pavilion, New York World's Fair, from *Architectural Forum*, vol. 70, n. 6, June 1939. Michele Busiri Vici (1894–1981), architect. G. E. K. Smith, photographer

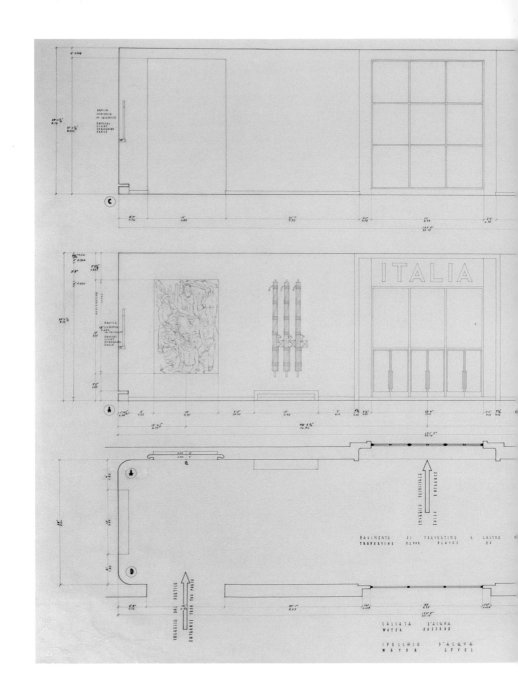

XLVIII.
Elevations and plan, *Italian Pavilion New York World's Fair 1939: Chief Entrance*, 1938.
Michele Busiri Vici (1894–1981)

84

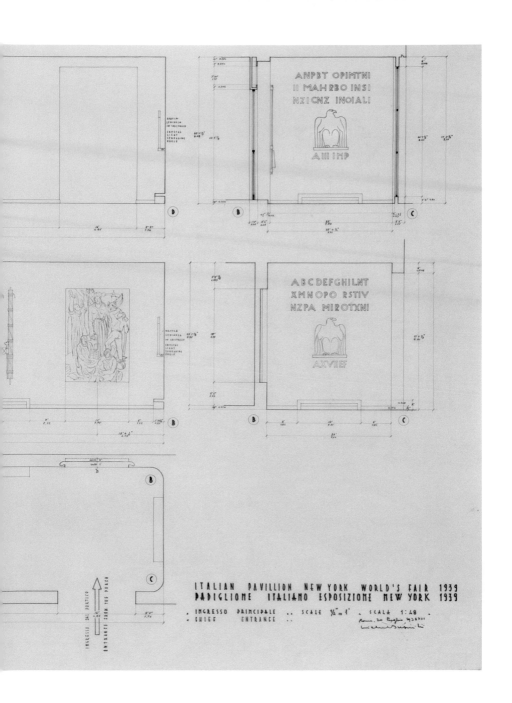

ITALIAN PAVILLION NEW YORK WORLD'S FAIR 1939
PADIGLIONE ITALIANO ESPOSIZIONE NEW YORK 1939

. INGRESSO PRINCIPALE .. SCALE ½"= 1' . SCALA 1:48
. CHIEF ENTRANCE ..

XLIX.
Perspective study, *Italian Pavilion New York World's Fair 1939: The Entrance Hall,*
1938. Michele Busiri Vici (1894–1981)

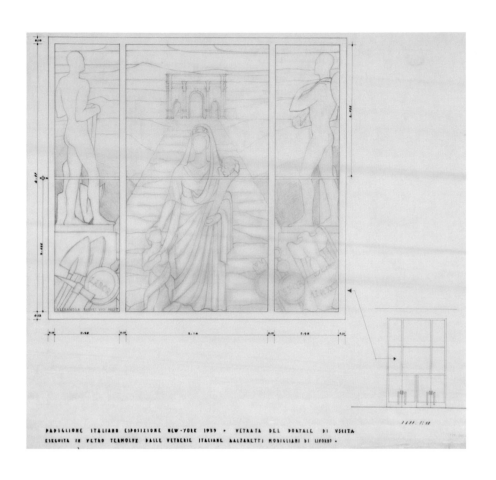

L.
Study, *Italian Pavilion New York World's Fair 1939: Glass Window of the Exit Portal*,
c. 1938. Alexandra (Assia) Olsoufieff Busiri Vici (1906–1989), designer

LI.
Sculpture, *Ritratto di Paola Ojetti*, 1935. Antonio Berti (1904–1990).
Fonderia Marinelli, Florence, foundry

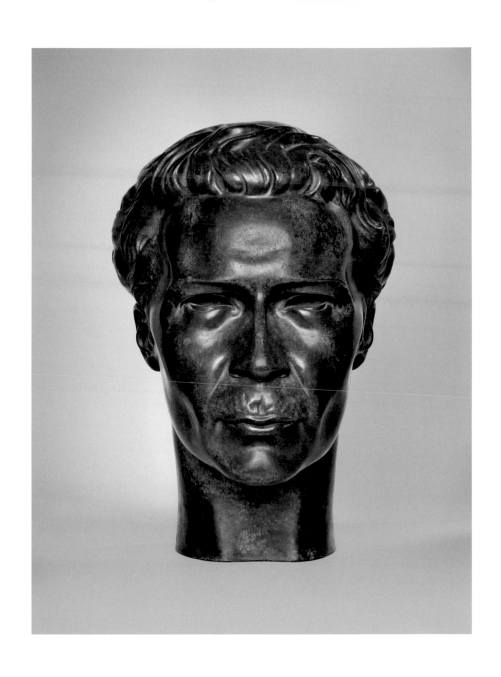

LII.
Sculpture, *Nicola Bonservizi*, 1925. Adolfo Wildt (1868–1931)

ILLUSTRATIONS & PLATES

All works from The Wolfsonian–FIU,
The Mitchell Wolfsonian, Jr. Collection,
unless otherwise noted.

Fig. 1

Periodical page 24, Renovation project for
the Augusteo, from *Capitolum*, vol. 1,
n. 1, April 1925
Marcello Piacentini (Italian, 1881–1960),
architect
Bestetti & Tumminelli, Milan, Rome,
publisher
The Wolfsonian–FIU, Gift of Greg Castillo,
XB1990.2200

Fig. 2

Pamphlet page 27, Augusteo as seen from
Corso Umberto, from *La sistemazione
della zona Augustea* (The Rearrangement
of the Augustean Zone), 1927
Enrico Del Debbio (Italian, 1891–1973),
architect
Federazione Fascista dell'Urbe, Rome,
publisher
TD1990.289.29

Fig. 3

Book page 105, *Documentazione
fotografica delle più importanti
opere di trasformazione edilizia e di
sistemazione archeologica volute dal
Duce per il maggiore splendore di
Roma* (Photographic Documentation of
the Most Important Works of Building
Transformation and Archaeological
Rearrangement Desired by the Duce for
the Greater Glory of Rome), c. 1938
Governatorato di Roma, Rome, publisher
XB1991.301

Fig. 4

Drawing, View of the Mole Adriana, 1934
Giannino Marchig (Italian, 1897–1983)
Graphite on paper
13 ⅞ x 19 ¼ in (35.2 x 48.9 cm)
XX1990.2404

Fig. 5

Periodical page 92, View of the plastic model
for the final approved rearrangement of
the Augustean zone, from special issue,
Architettura, 1936
Vittorio Morpurgo (Italian, 1890–1966),
architect
Fratelli Treves, Milan, publisher
84.3.17

Fig. 6

Periodical page 96, Detail of the plastic
model showing *Il Mito di Roma* (The Myth
of Rome) on the facade of the National
Institute for Social Security, from special
issue, *Architettura*, 1936
Vittorio Morpurgo (Italian, 1890–1966),
architect
Fratelli Treves, Milan, publisher
84.3.17

Fig. 7

Photograph of Ferruccio Ferrazzi with his
cartoon for *Tevere* (Tiber), from *Il Mito di
Roma* (The Myth of Rome), 1940
Gelatin silver print
9 x 6 ¾ in (22.9 x 17.1 cm)
XX1989.200.7

Fig. 8

Photograph of Ferruccio Ferrazzi's
daughters with his cartoon for *Aurora*,
from *Il Mito di Roma* (The Myth of Rome),
1940
Gelatin silver print
9 ⅛ x 6 ⅞ in (23.2 x 17.5 cm)
XX1989.200.8

Fig. 9

Photograph showing *L'Aurora* (Aurora) and
La Nascita (The Birth), from Ferruccio
Ferrazzi's cycle of frescoes in the
mausoleum of the Villa Ottolenghi, Acqui
Terme, 1953–57
Image courtesy of Archivio Ferrazzi, Rome

Fig. 10

Photograph of the Foro Mussolini under
construction, 1932
Romolo Del Papa (Italian), photographer
Gelatin silver print
7 ⅛ x 9 ⅜ in (18.1 x 23.8 cm)
XX1990.4037.4

Fig. 11

Book page 46, "Forum Mussolini:
Marmorstadion" (Marble Stadium), from
*Das Rom Mussolinis: Rom als moderne
Hauptstadt* (Mussolini's Rome: Rome as
a Modern Capital), 1943
Sepp Schüller (German), author and
photographer
Mosella-Verlag, Dusseldorf, publisher
XC2002.09.2

Fig. 12
Photograph of the marble stadium and the Academy of Physical Education, Foro Mussolini, c. 1937
George Hoyningen-Huene (American, b. Russia, 1900–1968), photographer
Gelatin silver print
9 ½ x 9 ½ in (24.1 x 24.1 cm)
XX1990.2666

Fig. 13
Menu cover, *Rex*, c. 1936
Ubaldo Cosimo Veneziani (Italian, 1894–1958), cover design
Edizioni Propaganda Italia – Lloyd Triestino – Adriatica – Tirrenia, publisher
XB1991.1868.11

Fig. 14
Book page 43, "Foro Mussolini: l'innalzamento del monolito di Carrara" (Foro Mussolini: The Raising of the Monolith of Carrara), from *Il nuovo volto d'Italia* (The New Face of Italy), c. 1933
Axel von Graefe (German, 1900–), photographer
Mondadori, Milan, publisher
TD1990.61.23

Fig. 15
Book page spread, Model of the exposition grounds, from *Esposizione Universale di Roma* (Universal Exposition of Rome), 1939
Pizzi & Pizio, Milan and Rome, printer
TD1990.89.12

Fig. 16
Medal, *Roma Aeterna – Esposizione Universale Roma, 1942-XX* (Eternal Rome – Universal Exposition Rome, 1942-Year Twenty of the Fascist Revolution), c. 1939
Aluminum
1 ¼ in dia. (3.2 cm dia.)
XX1991.646

Fig. 17
Postcard, View of the Italian Pavilion at Chicago World's Fair, 1933
C. R. Childs Company, Chicago, photographer
XC1991.170.271

Fig. 18
Photograph of the Restaurant Conte di Savoia inside the Italian Pavilion at the 1939 New York World's Fair
Image courtesy of Archivio N. Pulitzer, Bassano del Grappa

I.
Poster, *Tramvie del Governatorato* (Tramways of the Governorate), 1927
Ente Nazionale Industrie Turistiche (ENIT), publisher
Barabino & Graeve, Genoa, printer
Offset lithograph
41 x 29 ⅛ in (104.1 x 74.0 cm)
87.551.4.1

II.
Poster, *Roma. Mercato di Traiano* (Rome. Trajan's Market), c. 1930
Vittorio Grassi (Italian, 1878–1958), designer
Ente Nazionale Industrie Turistiche (ENIT), publisher
A. Marzi, Rome, printer
Offset lithograph
39 ½ x 25 in (100.3 x 63.5 cm)
XX1990.1808

III.
Poster, *Alle Wege führen nach Rom* (All Roads Lead to Rome), 1937
Severo (Sepo) Pozzati (Italian, 1895–1983), designer
Ente Nazionale Industrie Turistiche (ENIT), publisher
Coen & Co., Milan, printer
Offset lithograph
39 ½ x 24 ⅜ in (100.3 x 61.9 cm)
TD1990.34.3

IV.
Poster, *3 Ore Funivia Aquila Gran Sasso* (3 Hour Cableway Aquila Gran Sasso), 1934 (designed 1932)
Umberto Noni (Italian), designer
Barabino & Graeve, Genoa, printer
Offset lithograph
41 ⅛ x 29 ¼ in (104.5 x 74.3 cm)
87.533.4.1

V.
Pamphlet cover, *Rome*, 1933
Ente Nazionale Industrie Turistiche (ENIT),
  publisher
The Mitchell Wolfson, Jr. Collection
  of Decorative and Propaganda Arts,
  Promised Gift, WC2010.1.16.4

VI.
Pamphlet cover, *Rome*, 1936
Ente Nazionale Industrie Turistiche (ENIT),
  publisher
The Mitchell Wolfson, Jr. Collection
  of Decorative and Propaganda Arts,
  Promised Gift, WC2010.1.16.6

VII.
Poster, *Roma*, c. 1939
Ente Nazionale Industrie Turistiche (ENIT),
  publisher
Pizzi & Pizio, Milan and Rome, printer
Offset lithograph
39 ½ x 26 ¼ in (100.3 x 66.7 cm)
TD1990.34.4

VIII.
Model, Layout of the mausoleum in the
  Villa Ottolenghi at Acqui Terme, c. 1930
Marcello Piacentini (Italian, 1881–1960),
  architect
Plaster
12 x 55 x 42 ½ in (30.5 x 139.7 x 108.0 cm)
XX1989.3

IX.
Study for *Il Mito di Roma* (The Myth of Rome)
  with detail of building façade, 1940
Ferruccio Ferrazzi (Italian, 1891–1978),
  artist
Vittorio Morpurgo (Italian, 1890–1966),
  architect
Tempera, graphite, and pastel on paper
69 ¾ x 44 in (177.2 x 111.8 cm)
XX1989.200.1

X.
Study for *Il Mito di Roma* (The Myth of
  Rome) with detail of balcony, 1940
Ferruccio Ferrazzi (Italian, 1891–1978)
Tempera and pastel on paper
48 ¾ x 13 ⅝ in (123.8 x 34.6 cm)
XX1989.200.5

XI.
Cartoon, *Tevere* (Tiber), from *Il Mito
  di Roma* (The Myth of Rome), 1940
Ferruccio Ferrazzi (Italian, 1891–1978)
Tempera on paper
248 ¼ x 127 ½ in (630.6 x 323.9 cm)
XX1989.200.2

XII.
Photograph, Detail of Tiber, Romulus, and
  Remus, from the mosaic *Il Mito
  di Roma* (The Myth of Rome) by
  Ferruccio Ferrazzi, 1940
Gelatin silver print
9 ⅜ x 7 in (23.8 x 17.8 cm)
XX1989.200.9

XIII.
Photograph, Detail of the she-wolf, from
  the mosaic *Il Mito di Roma* (The Myth
  of Rome) by Ferruccio Ferrazzi, 1940
Gelatin silver print
9 ¼ x 7 in (23.5 x 17.8 cm)
XX1989.200.11

XIV.
Cartoon, *Aurora*, from *Il Mito di Roma*
  (The Myth of Rome), 1940
Ferruccio Ferrazzi (Italian, 1891–1978)
Tempera on paper
80 ⅜ x 132 in (204.2 x 335.3 cm)
XX1989.200.3

XV.
Photograph, Detail of Aurora, from the
  mosaic *Il Mito di Roma* (The Myth
  of Rome) by Ferruccio Ferrazzi, 1940
Gelatin silver print
6 ⅞ x 9 ¼ in (17.5 x 23.5 cm)
XX1989.200.6

XVI.
Cartoon, *Vesta*, from *Il Mito di Roma*
  (The Myth of Rome), 1940
Ferruccio Ferrazzi (Italian, 1891–1978)
Tempera on paper
118 ½ x 57 ⅜ in (301.0 x 145.7 cm)
XX1989.200.4

XVII.
Viewbook, *Il Foro Mussolini*, c. 1937
E. Verdesi, Rome, publisher
86.19.551

XVIII.
Book page 2, Overview of the Foro
  Mussolini, from *Progetti di costruzioni*
  (Construction Projects), 1928
Enrico Del Debbio (Italian, 1891–1973),
  author and architect
Opera Nazionale Balilla, Rome, publisher
84.2.333

XIX.
Photograph, Foro Mussolini under
  construction, 1932
Romolo Del Papa (Italian), photographer
Gelatin silver print
7 ⅛ x 9 ⅜ in (18.1 x 23.8 cm)
XX1990.4037.1

XX.
Photograph, Foro Mussolini under
  construction, 1932
Romolo Del Papa (Italian), photographer
Gelatin silver print
7 ⅛ x 9 ⅜ in (18.1 x 23.8 cm)
XX1990.4037.2

XXI.
Photograph, Foro Mussolini under
  construction, 1932
Romolo Del Papa (Italian), photographer
Gelatin silver print
7 ⅛ x 9 ⅜ in (18.1 x 23.8 cm)
XX1990.4037.3

XXII.
Photograph, Raising of the monolith of
  Carrara, Foro Mussolini, 1932
Romolo Del Papa (Italian), photographer
Gelatin silver print
7 ⅛ x 9 ⅜ in (18.1 x 23.8 cm)
XX1990.4036

XXIII.
Maquette, *La vela* (The Sail), c. 1933
For a Statue in the Foro Mussolini, Rome
Eugenio Baroni (Italian, 1880–1935)
Bronze
22 x 7 ⅞ x 7 ⅛ in (56.0 x 20.0 x 18.0 cm)
Wolfsoniana-Fondazione Regionale per
  la Cultura e lo Spettacolo, Genoa,
  87.1074.6.1

XXIV.
Maquette, *Fanciullo con cartiglio* (Young
  Boy with Scroll), c. 1933
For a statue in the Foro Mussolini, Rome
Aldo Buttini (Italian, 1898–1957)
Bronze
21 ¼ x 9 ⅞ x 7 ⅛ in (54.0 x 25.0 x 18.0 cm)
Wolfsoniana-Fondazione Regionale per
  la Cultura e lo Spettacolo, Genoa,
  GX1993.236

XXV.
Poster, *1a leva artistica della G. I. L.*
  (First Art Benefit for the G. I. L.),
  c. 1942
Filippo Romoli (Italian, 1901–1969),
  designer
SAIGA, formerly Barabino & Graeve,
  Genoa, printer
Offset lithograph
38 ¾ x 26 ½ in (98.4 x 67.3 cm)
86.4.42

XXVI.
Photograph, Statue of the Balilla, Foro
  Mussolini, c. 1937
George Hoyningen-Huene (American,
  b. Russia, 1900–1968), photographer
Gelatin silver print
9 ½ x 9 ½ in (24.1 x 24.1 cm)
XX1990.2663

XXVII.
Photograph, Marble stadium, Foro
  Mussolini, c. 1937
George Hoyningen-Huene (American,
  b. Russia, 1900–1968), photographer
Gelatin silver print
9 ½ x 9 ½ in (24.1 x 24.1 cm)
XX1990.2665

XXVIII.
Photograph, The monolith of Carrara,
  Foro Mussolini, c. 1937
George Hoyningen-Huene (American,
  b. Russia, 1900–1968), photographer
Gelatin silver print
9 ½ x 9 ½ in (24.1 x 24.1 cm)
XX1990.2664

XXIX.
Poster, *Settimana del Balilla, 5–10 Dicembre
XIV, Genova* (Balilla Youth Movement
Week, December 5–10, Year Fourteen of
the Fascist Revolution, Genoa), 1935
C. M., designer
Barabino & Graeve, Genoa, printer
Offset lithograph
55 ⅛ x 39 ½ in (140.0 x 100.3 cm)
XX1990.2962

XXX.
Brochure cover, *9 jours en Italie* (9 Days
in Italy), 1934
Gruppi Universitari Fascisti, Ente Nazionale
Industrie Turistiche (ENIT), Italy,
publisher
The Mitchell Wolfson, Jr. Collection
of Decorative and Propaganda Arts,
Promised Gift, WC2010.1.16.9

XXXI.
Medal, *Opera Balilla A X*, 1932
Bronze
2 in dia. (5.1 cm dia.)
83.1.295

XXXII.
Perspective study, *La Città di Cemento*
(The Concrete City), c. 1919
Virgilio Marchi (Italian, 1895–1960)
Stabilimento per la Riproduzione Disegni
L. Bazzichelli, Rome, printer
Diazotype
39 ¼ x 27 ⅝ in (99.7 x 70.2 cm)
TD1989.65.1

XXXIII.
Perspective study, *Testata di ponte*
(Bridgehead), 1926
Virgilio Marchi (Italian, 1895–1960)
Diazotype
27 ⅛ x 23 ⅞ in (68.9 x 60.6 cm)
TD1989.65.5

XXXIV.
Perspective study, *Progetto di grande tramvia
elettrica di cintura a Roma* (Project for
Big Electrical Tramway around Rome),
c. 1927
Virgilio Marchi (Italian, 1895–1960)
Diazotype
19 ¾ x 35 ⅝ in (50.2 x 90.5 cm)
TD1989.65.2

XXXV.
Poster, *Roma 1942 XX. Esposizione
Universale* (Rome 1942 Year Twenty
of the Fascist Revolution. Universal
Exposition), 1939
Giorgio Quaroni (Italian, 1907–1960),
designer
Edizioni dell'Esposizione Universale,
Rome, publisher
SAIGA, formerly Barabino & Graeve,
Genoa, printer
Offset lithograph
41 x 28 ½ in (104.1 x 72.4 cm)
The Mitchell Wolfson, Jr. Collection
of Decorative and Propaganda Arts,
Promised Gift, WC2011.06.4.1

XXXVI.
Poster, *E.42. Esposizione Universale di
Roma. Planimetria Generale* (E.42.
Universal Exposition of Rome. General
Plan), 1939
Edizioni dell'Esposizione Universale,
Rome, publisher
Offset lithograph
37 ⅝ x 26 ⅞ in (95.6 x 68.3 cm)
86.4.16

XXXVII.
Elevation sketch, Palazzo della Civiltà
Italiana, c. 1937
Giovanni Guerrini (Italian, 1887–1972)
Graphite on paper
8 ⅝ x 5 ⅝ in (22.0 x 14.2 cm)
The Wolfsonian–FIU, Purchase, 2013.7.2

XXXVIII.
Elevation sketch, Palazzo della Civiltà
Italiana, c. 1937
Giovanni Guerrini (Italian, 1887–1972)
Charcoal on paper
8 ⅝ x 11 ⅜ in (22.0 x 29.0 cm)
The Wolfsonian–FIU, Purchase, 2013.7.3

XXXIX.
Plan sketch, Palazzo della Civiltà Italiana,
c. 1937
Giovanni Guerrini (Italian, 1887–1972)
Ink on paper
5 ½ x 4 ⅛ in (14.0 x 10.5 cm)
The Wolfsonian–FIU, Gift of Elizabetta
Colombo Guerrini, 2013.7.1

XL.

Study, *Le Origini di Roma* (The Beginnings of Rome), 1940–41
For the competition "Mosaic Decoration in the Hall of the Palazzo dei Congressi," E42, Rome
Alberto Salietti (Italian, 1892–1961)
Tempera on paper
12 ⅞ x 26 in (32.9 x 66.0 cm)
Wolfsoniana-Fondazione Regionale per la Cultura e lo Spettacolo, Genoa, GD2002.254.1

XLI.

Study, *L'Impero* (The Empire), 1940–41
For the competition "Mosaic Decoration in the Hall of the Palazzo dei Congressi," E42, Rome
Alberto Salietti (Italian, 1892–1961)
Tempera on paper
12 ⅞ x 26 in (32.9 x 66.0 cm)
Wolfsoniana-Fondazione Regionale per la Cultura e lo Spettacolo, Genoa, GD2002.254.2

XLII.

Study, *Rinascimento e Universalità della Chiesa* (Renaissance and Universality of the Church), 1940–41
For the competition "Mosaic Decoration in the Hall of the Palazzo dei Congressi," E42, Rome
Alberto Salietti (Italian, 1892–1961)
Tempera on paper
12 ⅞ x 26 in (32.9 x 66.0 cm)
Wolfsoniana-Fondazione Regionale per la Cultura e lo Spettacolo, Genoa, GD2002.254.3

XLIII.

Study, *Roma di Mussolini* (Mussolini's Rome), 1940–41
For the competition "Mosaic Decoration in the Hall of the Palazzo dei Congressi," E42, Rome
Alberto Salietti (Italian, 1892–1961)
Tempera on paper
12 ⅞ x 26 in (32.9 x 66.0 cm)
Wolfsoniana-Fondazione Regionale per la Cultura e lo Spettacolo, Genoa, GD2002.254.4

XLIV.

Periodical advertisement, from *New York Times*, sec. 8, May 5, 1939
New York Times Company, New York City, publisher
The Wolfsonian-FIU, Gift of Vicki Gold Levi, XC1991.93

XLV.

Elevations and section, *Italian Pavilion New York World's Fair 1939: View of the Backside, Principal View, Cross Section*, 1938
Michele Busiri Vici (Italian, 1894–1981)
Ink on tracing paper
28 x 72 in (71.1 x 182.9 cm)
XX1990.1738

XLVI.

Model, Italian Pavilion, New York World's Fair, 1939
Michele Busiri Vici (Italian, 1894–1981), architect
Painted wood
10 ⅜ x 10 x 16 ¼ in (26.5 x 25.5 x 41.4 cm)
Wolfsoniana-Fondazione Regionale per la Cultura e lo Spettacolo, Genoa, GX1993.231

XLVII.

Periodical page 456, View of the Italian Pavilion, New York World's Fair, from *Architectural Forum*, vol. 70, n. 6, June 1939
Michele Busiri Vici (Italian, 1894–1981), architect
G. E. K. Smith, photographer
Time, Inc., New York City, publisher
86.3.5.456

XLVIII.

Elevations and plan, *Italian Pavilion New York World's Fair 1939: Chief Entrance*, 1938
Michele Busiri Vici (Italian, 1894–1981)
Ink on tracing paper
32 x 51 ½ in (81.3 x 130.8 cm)
XX1990.1736

XLIX.

Perspective study, *Italian Pavilion New York World's Fair 1939: The Entrance Hall,* 1938
Michele Busiri Vici (Italian, 1894–1981)
Ink on tracing paper
32 x 34 in (81.3 x 86.4 cm)
XX1990.1734

L.

Study, *Italian Pavilion New York World's Fair 1939: Glass Window of the Exit Portal,* c. 1938
Alexandra (Assia) Olsoufieff Busiri Vici (Russian, 1906–1989), designer
Ink and graphite on tracing paper
25 x 26 ½ in (63.5 x 67.3 cm)
XX1990.1753

LI.

Sculpture, *Ritratto di Paola Ojetti,* 1935
Antonio Berti (Italian, 1904–1990)
Fonderia Marinelli, Florence, foundry
Bronze
26 ¾ x 18 ⅞ x 13 ¾ in (68.0 x 48.0 x 35.0 cm)
The Mitchell Wolfson, Jr. Collection
of Decorative and Propaganda Arts,
Promised Gift, ITC2004.6.25

LII.

Sculpture, *Nicola Bonservizi,* 1925
Adolfo Wildt (Italian, 1868–1931)
Bronze
22 ½ x 12 x 18 in (57.2 x 30.5 x 45.7 cm)
The Mitchell Wolfson, Jr. Collection
of Decorative and Propaganda Arts,
Promised Gift, WC2002.10.33.1